WINTER
IN EDEN

WINTER IN EDEN

Poems by
Robert Schultz

Loess Hills Books
Farragut & Parkersburg, Iowa
1997

Book composition by Ireland Design & Publishing, Cedar Falls, Iowa.

Published by: Loess Hills Books
                        an imprint of
                  Mid-Prairie Books
                  P.O. Box C
                  Parkersburg, Iowa 50665

ISBN 0-931209-67-6 cloth

ISBN 0-931209-68-4 paper

ACKNOWLEDGEMENTS

The author would like to thank the editors of the following publications, in which the following poems first appeared: *The Cumberland Poetry Review*: "Antarctica," 1-3; *First Things*: "In a Field of Weeds" and part two of "Firewood" (as "When Lilacs Shake"); *Hubbub*: "Chanticleer"; *The Hudson Review*: "Vietnam War Memorial, Night," "Black Velvet," and "Winter in Eden," Vol. 45, No. 1 (Spring 1992), "Snowlight," Vol. 42, No. 4 (Winter 1990), "In This Dark Pool, Our Marriage Bed," "January 1," and "Two or Three Dreams of Spring," Vol. 40, No. 4 (Winter 1988), "It is Not Yet Morning, But Morning Rises" and "Analysis," Vol. 39, No. 2 (Summer 1986), "When the Magnitude of the Possible Dawned," Vol. 37, No. 3 (Autumn 1984); *Trapeze:* "She Speaks to Her Husband, Asleep"; *The Virginia Quarterly Review*: "The Moths," "Antarctica" 1-7, "The Morning News," "Marriage Fires," and "Sight & Distance." "In Mourning," Copyright © 1980 by Robert Schultz, first appeared in *Thirtieth Year to Heaven*, an anthology (The Jackpine Press). "On Forsythia Overhanging a Slate Wall" and "Fire-Eater" are reprinted from *Vein Along the Fault*, a chapbook published in an edition of 100 by The Laueroc Press, Copyright © 1979 by Robert Schultz.

For Sally,
Schuyler, and Lucy

CONTENTS

I. Marriage Fires

II. Antarctica

III. The Spectrum of Fire

Therefore the Lord God sent him forth from the garden of Eden, to till the ground from which he was taken. He drove out the man; and at the east of the garden of Eden he placed the cherubim, and a flaming sword which turned every way, to guard the way to the tree of life.

—Genesis 3: 23-4

Le Paradis n'est pas artificiel
                              but is jagged,
For a flash,
            for an hour.
Then agony,
            then an hour,
                        then agony....

—Ezra Pound, *Canto XCII*

I.
MARRIAGE FIRES

WAKING

Smearings of light, remembrance of music,
Interludes of hover and veer,
Then dim unlikely shapes appear—

Sheer white curtains lift at the window
As breezes clatter through twisting leaves
Flashing green and white. A landscape gathers,

Birds begin, and we in our bed
Both plunge again into total loss, loss
Of ourselves in our lives.

MARRIAGE FIRES

Where on the spectrum of living fire
Do a man and woman walk this morning
Through woods above a shallow river
Late in March? In winter they dozed
And smouldered coolly, or flared inside
Like ice on skin, a flame that numbs.
The grass lay matted and bleached by snow,
And so did they. She painted their walls
To peach or lavendar, blocking the reach
Of clouds and plains, that white on white.
He travelled widely, books in his lap,
Sailing the floorlamp's pool of light.
They did not know they had been so sick,
But, convalescent, they slept together,
In each other's arms in separate dreams.

In the woods today the early blossoms
Shine like snow: bloodroot, snow drops,
Dutchman's breeches. The man and woman
Breathe cool air. They did not know
They had been asleep, but now
The sensation of slowly waking. The sky
Behind its lattice-work of empty branches
Starts to their eyes a different blue,
Like a run of music or sudden breeze
That lifts a curtain. Low bushes thrust out
Pointed leaves, green on one side,
Red on the other, little fires
Breaking out on the branch.

Which way shall they walk? The path
Divides. One trail rims a limestone bluff,
Climbing through cedars, then opens high
Where she wants to lead him, hand in hand.
She thinks of how the river looks,

Reflected sun from rippling shallows
Seeming to burn a thousand holes
In the world below. He wants to go down.
The other trail descends through hardwoods,
Skirting a creek. He remembers a pool
Where runoff floods have tumbled the rocks
And once he scooped up spheres of granite,
One in each hand, to strike together
And hear them ring. Though water flew,
He saw their spark, saw the arc that tracked
A glowing chip and smelled like smoke.
So they stand at the branch, each holding
In mind a different way. They do not know
Both end in fire.

SHE SPEAKS TO HER HUSBAND, ASLEEP

"Moonlight pearls on my breast like solder.
Hotter and hotter, the needlepoint glows
As sewn beads burn their pattern in—
A snowflake pattern, my newest gown.
The frozen ground of these perfect sheets
Is a skillet to me. The whole house seethes
With difficult heat, inconvenient dreams,
Our children twisting like spreading flames.
You burrow into your willful sleep.
I whisper deep in the well of your ear:
'I'm alive, I'm alive! Are you dead to me?'"

BLACK VELVET

Cars lunge into the city,
Four abreast and pushing seventy.

Night's seductions draw us in.
Red streaks glow where the sun has fallen

On blackened stacks. Glittering turrets
Blaze at evening, towers of commerce

Burly-shouldered and empty-eyed.
Lit apartments hang their gardens against the sky.

Traffic hums in its usual groove.
I glide with the others, homing through

Toward familiar rooms. Halfway there
The billboard rises. Its brilliant square

Presents a woman in evening dress
Reclining by two glasses, ice,

And the opened bottle. She fingers
Its neck. The gesture lingers

As her level gaze
Attracts my eyes.

Here, in public, in a private car,
Fill the scene with your own desire:

Ceremonial drinks, two voices rubbing
Like bow and string,

The alcohol whispering,
Senses, velvet, extending dark wings.

I wince at the wrong,
The same old come on,

Women arranged by men and dollars
In poses drawn from early masters.

But sweeping around this curve in the dark—
Her form suspended, a park

Erected among the buildings
That light the city, stacked and burning—

I always look, each nightly trip,
From shoulder to waist

To the dangerous swerve of the hip.

SNOWLIGHT

Snowlight drew him, something new
Having wrapped the usual fuss and clutter
With hushed simplicity. Bushes and rooftops
Billowed and shone. Cars sat hunched
In polished domes while unplowed streets
Tipped right and left. Against this white,
Bare trees threw out their rough, black arms,
Pointing with certainty who knows where.

In the cemetery, his nearest park,
Tombstones held white crests above
Each pair of dates. He walked between them
With eyes that ate the small red berries
On drifted wreaths. He forgot the time
As beauty fed him. But time had stopped
For his close inspection of raspberry
Canes in a small ravine, the dark red
Tubes daubed lightly with blue.

Then he saw the procession,
The long sedan on slickened bricks
Slowly descending. He stood by the narrow
Graveyard road and watched it pass.
He saw a woman through tinted glass,
Her veil pulled back. She held very still
And stared ahead. In front of her
A rusted dump truck, blade attached,
Pushed snow aside. In its box a man
In a red plaid shirt was shovelling hard,
Sowing her road with salt.

JANUARY 1

Snow on the ground since mid-November
But no deep plunges through zero yet.
Just weeks of sky pulled taut in sheets.
So we live our days, crush white underfoot,
See white overhead at chimney-height,
And sleep at night between two white sheets.
We sleep in blackness hard as ice,
Obsidian ice we might chip with flint
If we reached our arms to strike at its flanks.
But we keep our arms under heavy blankets
And tangle our warmth in a knot we know
That will hold until morning, hold until morning
Again and again as the white disc arcs
Degree by degree through its lens of sky
To sharper focus on hard, cold buds.

IN THIS DARK POOL, OUR MARRIAGE BED

In this dark pool, our marriage bed,
We dove all night while the temperature plunged
And our exhalations froze on windows.

Morning's light shone dully like ivory.
Every pane bristled thick with frost: chevrons,
Flame-shapes, coral, barbed-wire—

Hundreds of night forms shaken from air
And fastened here by pins of ice.
"Look at the woods." You point at trunks

Unmistakably scrawled on sparkling glass.
Beneath them patchworks of squares and wedges
Suggest a town, but dwarfed by ferns.

Above, collisions of thrusting crystals
Jam a small sky.
In every window the white ghosts climb.

It troubles me, so I look away.
But knuckles cannot rub from my eyes
Our world drawn flat and crystallized

In stretched perspective—a chaos or cosmos
I cannot tell; it glitters, opaque.
I finally answer, "It bothers me," then

Rub the bright pane with a freezing thumb
To open an eye-hole. Cold flames burn,
But a clear space shows. I kneel and look,

See the whitened yards, the buffeted houses,
Streets in grids as if perfect crystals.
I see them as if they are etched on glass.

Only scattered pines hold a dark
Blue light, their centers deep coves
Where the sparrows swim.

TWO OR THREE DREAMS OF SPRING

1.

I step out onto
The open porch,
The long waiting

Finally over.
An all night rain
Has melted the snow,

The glassy mounds,
And water stands
In stunned, brown grass.

The first mild
Breezes smell like earth.
The flowering crab

(Was it always there
In the center of the yard?)
Is already open!

I lean against
The wooden porch-rail,
Take a deep breath,

Then wake in the dark—
Rub a hole with my fist
On frosted glass,

Look out on drifts.

2.

I am out on the porch;
The long waiting
Is finally over.

Loose water pools
In greening grass.
The air smells of earth.

Warm breezes tangle
Purple lilacs,
Whitening crabs.

Can this be a dream?
I rap my knuckles
Hard on the rail.

It hurts; it is real.
Then I wake, look out—
Hunched shoulders

Of snow.

3.

On the far side of town
A thin, green fog—
The first split buds.

Nearer, a maple,
Its catkins hanging
Like Spanish earrings.

And the grass, having sipped
Its snowdrifts down,
Burns green as Ireland

While tulips burn
In their bed by the porch
An unearthly red,

A red that wounds
As a way to heal.
Can this be real?

Can this be real?

On Forsythia Overhanging a Slate Wall

Forsythia sprawls from a central bang.
Branches arc like delight, as if to map
Trajectories of the heart. When the sap
Knocks in its pipes, the yellow blossoms swing
Like suns, brief trumpets loud with their light
Squeezed out from a branch of the void. Suns cool
Then drop like blossoms or cities into the pool
That can't be ruffled and reflects no light.

This bush shows how, by resistance, lives are built.
Forsythia—slow fountain—drills for the heart,
Taps capillary rills, and pumps rich silt,
Finds rhymes in the leaves' green labs, knots dirt
And sunlight tight, and over this slate wall
Slows water to a lobed and tendrilled fall.

THE MOTHS

Asleep in our lives, we wandered out
With trowel, lantern, and yellow dishpan,
Digging ferns in the hilly woods.
We imagined only a corner garden
Shaded in pines, as spring in the trees
Tipped quickly toward summer,
Afternoon sliding hard toward dusk.
Our pant-legs soaked in matted leaves,
Cold against clay, as we silently dug
Green fiddlehead scrolls and lacy fans,
Packing curled roots and handfuls of dirt
In the plastic tub. With evening settling,
I did not see the red of your cheeks.
When we stood again, you cradled
The pan of ferns in your arms, a small
Primordial world. I lit the gas lantern
And light jumped out in a hissing sphere
Among the dark trunks. Slim black wands,
Their shadows waved as the lantern swung
And we picked our difficult way toward home.
Then moths appeared, white flakes adrift
At the edge of light, but circling in
With hard, black eyes.
                              Now, in darkness,
The stunned-by-death waver hungrily out
Toward points of light. They swarm to us
In our brilliant globe, seeking blood-warmth,
Touch, a lick of our flame, one brush
Of your cheek, one singe.

FIREWOOD

1.

I think I'll cut
Some firewood down
For the windy night
When pines will wave
Like metronomes,
And we, by the fire,
In the knot we tie
So sweetly now,
Let frost-wires
Fasten the windows
Tight, content within
With our various flames.

2.

Now, in April, when lilacs shake
In gusts of rain, the crown-like buds
Waving thick and green on sceptre tips,
I ask myself: What have we been,
We two curled tight in winter's dark?

And when lilacs fully unfurl themselves,
Their heart-shaped leaves,
Their fragrant towers, purple or white,
Then what will we be
And what can we do as recklessly?

It Is Not Yet Morning, But Morning Rises

It is not yet morning, but morning rises
In dreaming eyes, though strangely

Vast, and a morning like evening.
In dream I attend to the changing sky

And its rustling sound, its rasping
Dry and tindery sound, like autumn leaves.

It is not the sound of autumn leaves,
But a change in the sky, some final stress

Of extremest weather, or of weather's end.
Then lines appear like veins of leaves

On the high, cold blue, and shards of it slip
To wheel in the air, careening the way

Bright leaves drift down. I watch the sky
Shift steadily down with emptying eyes,

Leaving blankness there, a whiteness not light—
The air, the blue, all dimension gone.

Then I wake in a room I have never seen,
In an unknown world, though my own.

Familiar birds sing familiar songs,
But differently now, from trees whose whispers

Arouse the doubts that pilgrims know
When they step at first onto newfound land.

II.
ANTARCTICA

ANTARCTICA

1.

As we step toward the perfect Antarctic,
Green at first, but deliberate in our hatred,
Which keeps us marching, we are struck
After every kill by the spots of red
On the snow, by the splash on porcelain.
Red, which seems so impossible, wrapped
In the snow of a gull or seal, burgeons
When metal fingers the passion trapped
Inside. Besides these sudden gushings, darkness
And light in various shades of brilliance, haze,
Diffusion, lustre, and utter absence comprise
The antarctic palette. Our balancing trick
Is to walk this narrow spectrum, our eyes
Vacant, missing nothing, not glancing back.

2.

Vacant, missing nothing, not glancing back,
We march the plains of porcelain, chrome,
Formica, glass, and polished tiles that crack
When the temperature dives. It's just like home.
At night cold fixtures gleam in the snowy light,
Planets freeze in their tracks, and zero
Pinches hard. I slept warm in my tight
Hell at home, icy with fears, burning to go.
Here, at least, we acknowledge imminent
Failure, the emptiness even of reaching
The pole, of seeing the compass spin; we cling
To hatreds: willful, petty, and nearly spent,
They have brought us here, from plains as stinging
And vast, which we paced in our own apartments.

Stinging and vast, paced in small apartments
Or here on an icy continent, difficult plains
Must be crossed. Try to live on dazzle lent
Desolation solely by light on snow: pain
Itself can fuel ecstatic dancing, but only
Briefly. Borrow the nighttime sky, or snow-blind
Walk in more perfect darkness, stepping carefully:
Absence in such magnitude seems sublime.
The sun's cool million candles burn sight down
To its charcoal root. Darkness gapes at noon
On the floes, each man in a night of his own.
The black sun pings, its echoes, metallic,
All there is for a man with his eyes unlit.
I reach out my arms. There is nothing; I see it.

4.

I reach into nothing, seeing it briefly—
Caverns of absence behind the folds
Of a world that goes. What does not go
Stays here: self in the dark, now accurately
Snouted with lusts, or clawed and toothed
With anger that grows in sickles back into flesh.
Here is the hell of a just inheritance;
This I can say is mine: midnight at noon
On ice at my southern pole. The whole cold
Continent rocks when I drop to my knees,
Too late for contrition, too soon for release
Into anything else, but speared on the old
Two prongs of remorse and what might have been
In a temperate zone with patches of green.

5.

Patches of green in a temperate zone,
In apparition, refresh closed eyes long
Scalded by winter light. The permafrost
Unlocks cool springs to water the acres,
Transfiguring ice to an Iowa lush
With its crops—or fountains in cities
Announce a flowering close by the streets.
I would walk where the buildings repeat
Wild gestures of upward reach, or trees
Contend for their swaths of blue. In the hush
They hold between night and day they might shelter
Us, who have failed here once. Self-exiled and lost,
We watch for the cleft where we might belong
Through a pane of ice, in fever, alone.

6.

In fever alone might this pane of ice
Melt back from my face, the chill recede,
And the scent of grass be paradise.
Illness heats; I can hear the buried seeds
Burst, scattering feelers in loosened ground
And probing their stems through the crust above
To fix on the sun. New leaves conduct their green
Transactions as fruitage begins. Soon cloves
Of oranges circle their hubs in orchards
Or bowls, or heaped in crates under awnings
Painted in tropical stripes. Even in yards
Where undergrowth jabs, bright globes still balance
The riot beneath—the tangled reachings
We chose to leave for a polished expanse.

7.

We chose to leave for this polished expanse
And must lunge out of visions to shivering
Dogs and sloping plains where glaciers advance.
Where we stop to drink the iceworm swims
In its cut-glass bowl; when we march again
Our frozen breaths—small clouds of needles—
Glitter in air and disperse. The pains
We have husbanded now appear useless,
Mere crowns of frost. As even the iciest
Beauty goes, and truth begins to encroach,
We try and fail to read the story as comic.
Absolute zero, the point at which we must
Stop and vanish, attends our approach
As we step toward the perfect Antarctic.

III.
THE SPECTRUM OF FIRE

IN A FIELD OF WEEDS

Man is but a reed, the weakest in
nature, but he is a thinking reed.

—Pascal, *Pensées*

Five degrees. Rough, shifting winds. Sunlight crashing
Almost audibly, sky to snow-pack, snow-pack to sky.
Eyes shrink hard to their smallest stop, but winter drills in.
Brilliant splinters of ice in the air blow up and down.

In the polished field stiff weeds poke through like rusty wire.
Stems and branches, anchored in ice, shake hard with gusts,
Knock stalk on stalk and litter the snow with broken reeds.
Detritus lifts in a whirl of air, then lies back down.

Hollow weeds rattle bone on bone, and the man who listens
Slowly turns to scan the rim of an icy zero. Acres of snow
Reach every way. Sunlight fills the blinding page.
He has come out here to read what it says, and he thinks he knows.

He walks back home and remembers everything;
Everything holds in his icy mirror. When words arrive
He chooses those which fabricate nothing, take nothing away.
I read the words on the snowy page and they stick like burrs.

They name the terror and make it flower. We stand together.

THE MORNING NEWS

This is how the future arrives:
The radio crackles three hundred dead,
A great heart holds their cancelled lives

In brilliant air, the public grieves,
Then the next blow comes. Our nerves go bad,
But this is how the future arrives.

Morning by morning the planet dives
From dark to light still sheathed in blood.
Some great heart may hold their lives,

But we did not know them, husbands and wives
Who plunged last night to a final bed.
This is how the future arrives

And we fight it off. We cannot give
Ourselves to them, can only plead
That some great heart hold all their lives.

A nearing moment balanced on knives
Points hard at us. It is dressed in red.
This is how the future arrives.
May some great heart hold all our lives.

In Mourning

The complex leaf
Of a potted palm
Lifts me clear of the chattering

Into the risings
Of each of her parts in the fruit tree,
Grasses and fern.

I think of the poise
Of an apple filling,
The body that turns, remote;

But only a stack of hollow bones
Can hold the juice
So hot with this love:

Electrical, quick,
And bright in the dark,
It leaps to unite

Seer and seen,
Lover and beloved.
O sister, forgive me for speaking

This language of disease, of parts
Which break: blood and heart
That swing in a gallows of bones.

Sores in the mouth
Taste like nails; cancer builds
Its city inside.

Yet this is the world which still
Pretends to offer a garden:
Desert apples, a circle of hills,

Spikenard and saffron,
Calamus, aloes—
All the chief spices

And water running with light on its back
By the palm, the almonds,
The gathering hands.

Where is this garden?
We dream of repose,
Of an apple, broken,

Filling with light.

WINTER IN EDEN

There are no fences, no gates in the snowy
Fields and wrecked orchards; only the sword-blade

Winter light swings north to south, east to west
Where the straight horizon locks itself with ice

To a sky too bright to look at. We are free
Among the trees of knowledge, gleaning

Shrivelled apples and berries, sweet
As they melt in our hot mouths. Memory

Flares as we walk beneath the torn limbs.
At home each night the dream arrives, insistent

As a chanted word: the slim trunk rises,
Branches dense with scalloped leaves protecting

Their fruit—globes the colors of perfect bodies,
Naked, shameless in the tree of life.

CHANTICLEER

Chanticleer in the unchinked cabin
Cries this morning: "I desire to speak
In a waking moment to those awake."

"Sit in my doorway and watch with me:
The fire-ball sun climbs the pine tree rungs.
Night mists lift from the pond like veils."

"Throw off the sleep that veils your eyes.
We could entertain a goddess here,
Auroral all day with a dawning in us."

He ends his call—"Wake up! Wake up!"—
As the sun cuts through.
     I hide my face.
The light that puts out sight is darkness.

SIGHT & DISTANCE

Afternoon like a crystal box: pine trees,
    citizens, rising clouds
      in shining cases.

Finches dart through walnut branches,
    through scissoring light,
Specimens perfect, air like glass.

But I'm all eyes and no hands—
Things flash and recede.

The sun goes down and evening buffs
    its copper brighter.

Lights snap on at the tops of poles
And insects madden, circling globes.

Bats and swallows veer and feed,
    veer and feed,
As night hawks dive, their gullets open.

Dark descends to gorge itself on the gorgeous Earth.

Darling, touch me. I'm almost here.

FIRE-EATER

On the sun the fiery towers hurtle up;
Bright arcs billow and split,
Blown by genial rage.

The Earth answers
Mildly. Its green corona
Shines on the hills.

And who is happier than I am,
Browsing the lettuces, tasting
The cooled, brittle flames?

ANALYSIS

Hefting the axe-head,
Throwing it down through
Oak's red heart,

I wonder and swing,
The wide blue day opening
Worlds within worlds

In winter branches,
In shadowy centers
Of boxwood shrubs

Where the quick eye lingers,
Curious after the hidden
Root of what it sees

And hardly believes:
A globe of living forms
Afloat in glittering air.

The steel head cleaves
Fragrant slabs from rounds,
Uncasking intoxicants—

Wood's bouquet like
Burgundy aged
In the innermost rings.

Slabs clatter;
Kindling splits
With a few more strokes;

But still red oak holds
Tight in its grain
A bottomless space

Where planets swish
And imagination dives in vain
For grounding or platform.

Meanwhile, back in the bluish
Light of early December,
Two imparadised birds

Are whistling, hidden in pines,
And deep inside a whorl
Of hardwood, blade against burl,

The axe-head rests.
I pry and hammer, pry
'Til the splitting handle snaps,

Then carry the whole
With its swallowed wedge
Back home to my grate,

Where the knot I could not
Break with my axe,
The fire unties.

Vietnam War Memorial, Night

To the left the spotlit Washington Monument
Jabs the air, progenitive, white;
Beyond trees, to the right, the stonework glows
Where Lincoln broods in his marble seat;

And here, between, in the humid dark,
Where curving pathways lead and branch,
Sally and I step forward carefully
Somewhere near the open trench.

Choppers shuttle across the sky
With jets for National crying down,
But we've lost our way. The intricate dark
In the center of town moves all around.

There are others here: white T-shirts drift
In heavy air. Then three bronze soldiers
Caught in floodlights across the field
Stare hard at where we want to go.

From above we find the wall's far end
And begin to descend. Ahead of us
Soft footlights brush the lustered stone,
Dim figures trace their hands across

The rows of letters, and others, hushed,
File past in the dark. At first we are only
Ankle deep in the names of the dead,
But the path slopes down. Quietly,

We wade on in. In the depths beside
The lit inscription, men and women
Hold each other, mortal, drowning.
Many have stopped at a chosen station

To touch an absence carved away.
From deep inside the chiselled panels
Particular deaths rush out at them.
The minds of veterans gape like tunnels

To burning huts. We are over our heads.
Now Sally turns, sobs hard, and stops.
We cling to each other like all the rest
And climb away with altered steps.

WHEN THE MAGNITUDE OF THE POSSIBLE DAWNED

1.

Last night we were lost. This morning
The back yard argues, as ever,
All pain is minor and passing.
Solid light, in its blocks and slabs,
Displaces vague fears, the night
Benign, domestic beneath trim shrubs.
By this light I'm stripping wild vines
From the plum, while its blossoms
Snow and the vines haul back, perverse
And muscular, tearing at last.
The grass throbs brighter the deeper
I breathe, and the season burns.
How surely the year finds its way
Toward spring, where Sally kneels
In the lettuce rows, a streak of clay
Like rouge on one cheek. Beside her
Schuyler careens and falls, inspects
A red clod, and rises again, his face
Aglow from within. So the day
Wheels by. And I am the watchful
Husbandman at evening here on a spinning
Ball when the green lawns tilt and night
Spills out from hedges and trees.

2.

In dissolving night, when all is possible,
Sky a caldron of stars distending
To spew the planets or melt them down,
The lights of creation and decreation
Sparkle inseparably. Here by my son,
While rapid creepers retake the plum
And Sally pitches in troubled sleep,
I keep my watch

Through dangerous hours
When the night light's glow
Throws a nimbus about
My viral, incendiary boy.

His hot skin burns me.
Asleep, he leans in a sprinter's pose
While I kneel on the floor,
Sponging him down from l04.

This bomb is smart,
Homing its fire to the heart.

Bare on the Earth in this little room
Where the moment crests and I waken
Anew, again and again,
What may not happen?

Pray without ceasing.

*

Bless Aaron Bobb,
Who, my son's age,
Has died of a cancer
Strangling his heart.

Relieve his parents
Of their wildest rage
Which seeks an answer
Beyond all art.

3.

When the magnitude of the possible
Dawned—a morning doubly brilliant—
Many were so near they vanished instantly.
Others ran to the city's rivers, naked
But indistinguishable, woman from man.
As a black rain fell on the fires, the wounded
Dug for the buried wounded.

"Although we were lying side by side on the stairs,
We did not recognize each other.
He seemed unable to open his eyes or mouth
For the swelling of his burns, but he said somehow:
'Are you Mr. Matsumuro?' It was Yoshimoto,
And he knew me, too, when I spoke."

After the sickness and mourning, the spiking
Temperatures, bodily ruin unspeakable,
Grief and listlessness cupping the loss,
Survivors slipped out of gloves
Of themselves, sloughed off old surfaces,
Suffered grafts and reconstructions, and lived
With explosives buried inside.

4.

Especially after the acreage fires
The burr-oak thrives, its jack-box

Seeds tripped loose by the heat.
We tell ourselves such facts

As we can, to redeem charred waste,
And we note tough weeds scrabbling

Quick on a bank dozed clear.
The first mean vines knit up

A deep gouge, making soil for the next
Growth in line. New seeds more delicate follow,

Succession leading through pines
To beech, to this hardwood stand where

The shady floor is a powder of leaves,
Inviting and cool.

How spacious the bottomless sky
Appears from where I lie

In leafmeal and spines.
Trunks aim high toward the vanishing

Point where a star will appear
And tug all night on the buried dead.

By morning fingers, slender
And white, will have broken the loam.

Runners will leaf and at bushes
Or windfalls their tendrils loop

To entangle and climb,
To consume with a fire of their own.

Though soil is ash,
And I stretch myself over strata of bones,

Does the pea-vine climb less securely up?
Is the honeysuckle annulled?

I will rest myself in this undergrowth,
Serene as the ferns, the columbine, moss,

Clematis, and grass—as the whole
Unconscious world in which

The moment is full
And unhistorical.

5.

Out from this chapel, its green
Enfolding sacristy quieting
All it surrounds—the weavings
Of grass, composures of weeds,
The scent of mint from certain
Crushed leaves, above it all
Hypnotic wavings of trees acircle—
Out from this chapel yet something
Reaches from me toward my life
In the intricate flames of destruction
And love.

6.

Out from the oak in the fireplace grate
Heat and light uncoil in tongues,
Hissing their song of the Fortunate Man
Who rests by wife and child at home
While November gusts. Needles, leaves,
And bits of trash, finding their motion
In sudden whirlwinds, wander the streets.
The plum and its vine, now stripped and wiry,
Huddle their warmth in the naked yard.
I gaze out the window as night comes on;
Sally reads; Schuyler asks to poke the fire.
Sparks like souls ascend the dark shaft.

Beyond our most immediate air,
Behind the ridge at evening's edge, the sun
Ignites the sky at its hem, and the sheerest
Garment we know goes up. Sleeves of flame
Extend toward the zenith; clouds like ingots
Heat and glow. Even the icy cirrus burn,
Fanned into coals, irradiating the upper air
As our windows flare and the whole sky twists.

To live within this involving flame,
We must be fire. Sally, we live by burning
Slowly, and know ourselves best
When we recognize the banked up fires
In each other's eyes. I think of them
When the evening reddens, sky folding up
Like Earth's last day. It gathers me
And lets me go, a nightly memento.

NOTES

"Chanticleer" extracts a theme from *Walden*, absorbing many of Thoreau's phrases.

"When The Magnitude Of The Possible Dawned," part 3, draws from two newspaper articles and a book about the Hiroshima and Nagasaki bombings: "A Final Accounting of the Death and Destruction," by Kai Erikson, a review in the August 9, 1981 *New York Times Book Review* of *Hiroshima and Nagasaki: The Physical, Medical, and Social Effects of the Atomic Bombings*, by The Committee for the Compilation of Materials On Damage Caused by the Atomic Bombs in Hiroshima and Nagasaki, translated by Eisei Ishikawa and David L. Swain (New York: Basic Books, 1981); "The Bomb and the Remembering," by Liz Nakahara in the August 6, 1981 *Washington Post;* and *Unforgettable Fire: Pictures Drawn by Atomic Bomb Survivors*, ed. by Japan Broadcast Corporation (New York: Pantheon, 1981).

ABOUT THE AUTHOR

Robert Schultz is the author of a novel *The Madhouse Nudes* (Simon and Schuster, 1997) and a volume of poetry *Vein Along the Fault* (The Laueroc Press, 1979). His poetry, fiction and essays have appeared in *The Hudson Review, The Virginia Quarterly Review* and other journals. He was awarded the Emily Clark Balch Prize for Poetry from *The Virginia Quarterly Review* in 1988 and was a finalist for the Yale Younger Poets Prize in 1990. Schultz received his M.F.A. and Ph.D. degrees from Cornell University. He is Associate Professor in English at Luther College in Decorah, Iowa, where he lives with his wife Sally and children Schuyler and Lucy.